I LOVE ANIMALS

By Shelly Neilsen
Illustrated by Anastasia Mitchell

Published by Abdo & Daughters, 4940 Viking Drive Suite 622, Edina, Minnesota 55435.

Library bound edition distributed by Rockbottom Books, Pentagon Tower, P.O. Box 36036, Minneapolis, Minnesota 55435.

Edited by Julie Berg

LIBRARY OF CONGRESS CATALOGING-IN-PUBLICATION DATA

Nielsen, Shelly. 1958 -
    I love animals / written by Shelly Neilsen : [edited by Julie Berg].
       p.   cm. -- (Target Earth)
    Summary: Brief text and suggested activities introduce the importance of animals.
    ISBN 1-56239-191-7
    1. Animals -- Juvenile literature. 2. Pets -- Juvenile literature. [1. Animals. 2. Pets.] I. Berg, Julie. II. Title.   III. Series.
    QL49.N53 1993
    591--dc20
    [B]   93-18955
                                                              CIP
                                                              AC

 Thanks To The Trees From Which This Recycled Paper Was First Made.

I LOVE ANIMALS PLEDGE

I promise to love the animals. I'll treat them kindly, like my pals. I'll offer them water or a gentle word. I'm glad I'm a kid who loves the animals.

Look! Look! Animals! Fat ones, furry ones,
wild ones, tame ones. I'm glad animals live on
Earth. Animals and people belong together.
I love animals.

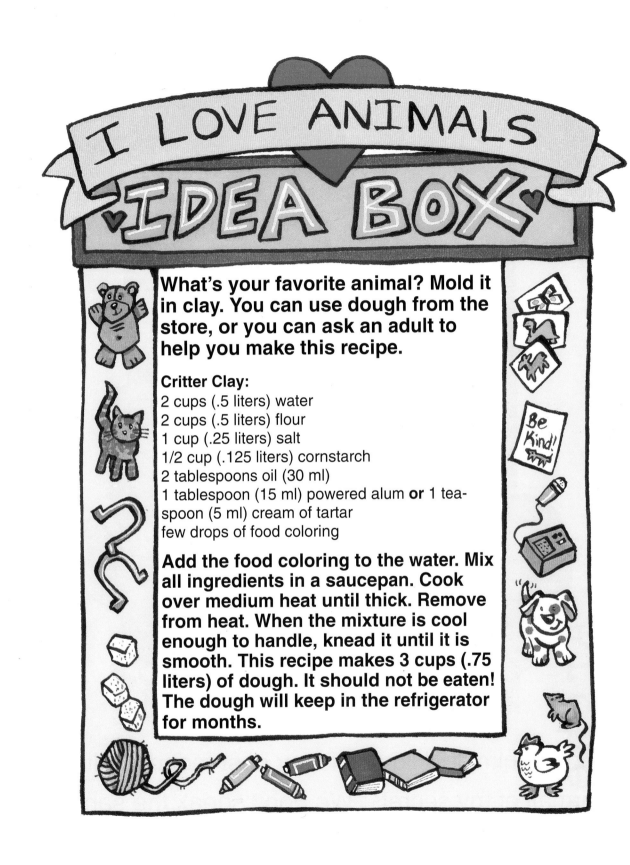

I LOVE ANIMALS IDEA BOX

What's your favorite animal? Mold it in clay. You can use dough from the store, or you can ask an adult to help you make this recipe.

Critter Clay:
2 cups (.5 liters) water
2 cups (.5 liters) flour
1 cup (.25 liters) salt
1/2 cup (.125 liters) cornstarch
2 tablespoons oil (30 ml)
1 tablespoon (15 ml) powered alum **or** 1 teaspoon (5 ml) cream of tartar
few drops of food coloring

Add the food coloring to the water. Mix all ingredients in a saucepan. Cook over medium heat until thick. Remove from heat. When the mixture is cool enough to handle, knead it until it is smooth. This recipe makes 3 cups (.75 liters) of dough. It should not be eaten! The dough will keep in the refrigerator for months.

Be Kind!

I love animals. Higgins is my best friend. I tell him all of my secrets. We don't speak the same language, but we understand each other. I love animals.

I LOVE ANIMALS IDEA BOX

Take a minute to show your pet that you care. A scratch behind the ears or a friendly word will make your pet's day!

I love animals. I wish I had a fat, brown horse who lived in my backyard. I'd brush her, feed her, and give her clean water to drink. I'd even let her nibble carrots from my hand. I love animals.

I LOVE ANIMALS IDEA BOX

If you don't have a horse in **your** backyard, you can keep a pretend horse. Throw the saddle on anytime and go for a gallop. Don't forget the sugar cubes!

I love animals. It's time for a game of pretend with my friends. I want to be the monkey because they hop and scratch. Cal is the deer because they run fast—fast—fast. And Helen pretends she's a hyena because they laugh and laugh. I love animals.

I LOVE ANIMALS

IDEA BOX

Make an animal mask. You will need a paper plate, paper punch, scissors, yarn, and markers or crayons. First, use the scissors to cut holes in the plate for your eyes and nose. Punch small holes on each side. Thread the holes with a piece of yarn. (Make a large knot on the end of the yarn so it doesn't pull through.) Decorate the mask with markers or crayons. What will you make? A lion? A bat? A cow? A walrus?

Be Kind!

I love animals, so I went on a friendly safari. I took a picture of a rabbit chewing lettuce... a cat sleeping on the sidewalk...and my little sister wearing a toy elephant trunk. She didn't count as an animal at all! I love animals.

I LOVE ANIMALS IDEA BOX

Go on a library safari to find books about animals you've never heard of. Did you discover any new creatures? What's an ocelot? A newt? An orangutan?

I love animals, so my friends and I did an animal dance. We stamped our hooves. We wagged our tails. We wiggled our ears, and shook our fur. We had so much fun, we never wanted to stop. I love animals.

I LOVE ANIMALS IDEA BOX

You can have an animal dance, too. Invite your friends. Choose the animals you will pretend to be. Will you dance like a gerbil? Or would you rather be a chicken? Start the music, and dance, you party animal, you!

I love animals. These kittens are brand new—
homemade by my grown-up cat, Mrs. Mittens.
They're soft and tiny. Their eyes are closed tight. I
can look all I want— but I'd better not touch! I love
animals.

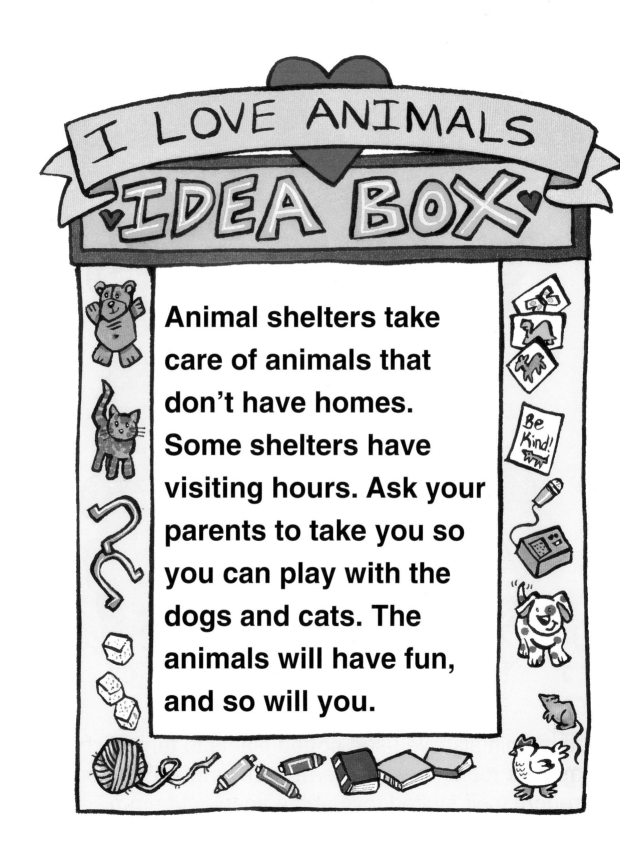

I LOVE ANIMALS

IDEA BOX

Animal shelters take care of animals that don't have homes. Some shelters have visiting hours. Ask your parents to take you so you can play with the dogs and cats. The animals will have fun, and so will you.

Be Kind!

I love animals. We used potted plants to turn my friend Jasper's room into a make-believe jungle. Everyone brought their stuffed toys and a snack. "Mmmm," said Barney, "pass the bananas." Sid said, "May I have a little more coconut ice cream, please?" What a wild jungle time. I love animals.

I LOVE ANIMALS
IDEA BOX

Make animal sounds with your friends. Record them on a cassette recorder. Can your family guess what kind of animals you are?

I love animals—even Roscoe, our class rat. He
needs fresh food and water every day. I always
give him an extra scratch on the back. Roscoe and
I are good buddies. I love animals.

I LOVE ANIMALS IDEA BOX

Talk to your friends and family. Tell them how to be kind to the Earth's animal friends. People need animals, and animals need people! We help each other.

Be Kind!

I love animals—from A to Z. All of these animals make the world wonderful. Anteaters. Baboons. Chimpanzees. Ducks. Elephants. Ferrets. Gazelles. Hippos. Iguanas. Jaguars. Kangaroos. Llamas. Mink. Nanny goats. Opossums. Panthers. Quails. Raccoons. Seals. Tigers. Unicorns. Vampire bats. Wombats. X-tra Wombats. Yaks. Zebras. I love animals.

I LOVE ANIMALS IDEA BOX

Make an animal alphabet border for your room. Here's how to do it. Tape sheets of paper together. Use markers or crayons to draw animals from A to Z. You will need help putting the border on your wall.

TARGET EARTH™ COMMITMENT

At Target, we're committed to the environment. We show this commitment not only through our own internal efforts but also through the programs we sponsor in the communities where we do business.

Our commitment to children and the environment began when we became the Founding International Sponsor for Kids for Saving Earth, a non-profit environmental organization for kids. We helped launch the program in 1989 and supported its growth to three-quarters of a million club members in just three years.

Our commitment to children's environmental education led to the development of an environmental curriculum called Target Earth™, aimed at getting kids involved in their education and in their world.

In addition, we worked with Abdo & Daughters Publishing to develop the Target Earth™ Earthmobile, an environmental science library on wheels that can be used in libraries, or rolled from classroom to classroom.

Target believes that the children are our future and the future of our planet. Through education, they will save the world!

TARGET®

Minneapolis-based Target Stores is an upscale discount department store chain of 517 stores in 33 states coast-to-coast, and is the largest division of Dayton Hudson Corporation, one of the nation's leading retailers.